What gives Zoe B

Fifty celebrities open their kitchens to share with us the joys of favourite family recipes, ranging from the ultra-healthy delights of Gary Lineker's Tofu Stir Fry, through Antony Worrall Thompson's gorgeous Grilled Scallops with Avocado-Corn Relish, to Michael Caine's calorific Carrot Cake.

Food fit for a king (or a prime minister, at least)...

So share the tastes of the rich and famous, helping youngsters who suffer from kidney disease as you do - because ALL the profits derived from sales of this book go to benefit research into kidney disease in babies and young children.

We'll help you to eat well. You'll help them to get well. What could be tastier than that?

Have you ever wondered how Judi Dench makes her bread and butter..?

Dedicated to :
Freddie, Claudia and Tara

Famous Family Food

Compiled by Julia Moross

The Book Guild Limited
Sussex, England

Acknowledgments

With thanks to:

- Amanda & Stephen Argent • Andrea Bartlett • Attenborough Associates Ltd • Carol Biss • Rory Byrne • Frances Edmonds
- Mayella Figgis • Trevor Gulliver • Gavin Krombas • Joff Lee
- Lark Masney • Helen McCabe • Andy Morris • Cindy & David Moross • Jennifer & Dominic Moross • Anne Mullins
- New Zealand Lamb • Susie Noble • Neil Reading • Alistair Ross
- Bridget Torlesse • Roxy & Mark Thornton • Richard Trompeter
- Janet Warren • David West-Nelson

For all recipes, quantities are given in both metric and imperial measures. Follow either set but not a mixture of both, because they are not interchangeable.

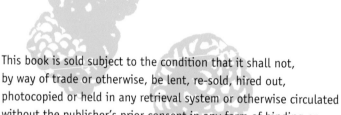

The Book Guild Ltd, 25 High Street, Lewes, Sussex

First Published 1999
© The Book Guild Ltd, 1999
Illustrations and design by Viccari Wheele Ltd, Hove
Origination printing and binding in Singapore under the supervision of MRM Graphics Ltd, Winslow, Bucks

A catalogue record for this book is available from the British Library

ISBN 1 85776 379 3

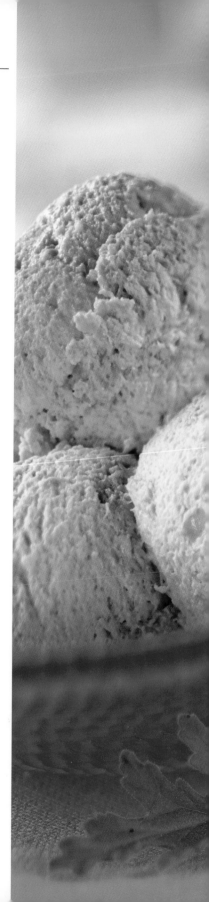

Foreword

There is no more compelling sound on earth than the cry of a child who needs you, and few children need your help more desperately than those with kidney disease.

The Institute of Child Health, which works in close conjunction with the Great Ormond Street Hospital for Children, carries out vital research into kidney disease in babies and children. KRAF (the Kidney Research Aid Fund) has been supporting this crucial work since 1973.

The issues and illnesses involved are many and varied, but the critical importance of good nutrition for infants and children with chronic renal failure cannot be overstated.

It is against this backcloth that KRAF decided to create a Celebrity Recipe Book. Celebrities from the media, music, sport and business have all generously contributed by sharing with us their favourite family meals. In many cases it is their children's favourite recipes that we feature.

Remember, KRAF is a charity with voluntary workers only.

There are no office overheads and no salaried staff, so the money raised from this Celebrity Recipe Book goes straight to those who need it .

To the many people who have helped in the creation of this compilation, KRAF would like to express its enormous gratitude. Thank you, also, for the support and generosity you have shown in buying this book. May it bring you a host of great meals in good company and more important still, the joy of knowing that you are helping some truly great little kids.

*Frances
Edmonds*

**Frances Edmonds,
London, 1998**

Dr. Richard S Trompeter

Introduction

The results of ante-natal ultrasound screening programmes indicate that approximately one in every five hundred babies may have a structural abnormality of one or both kidneys. Fortunately, the majority of these congenital abnormalities resolve spontaneously and are therefore not a problem for the baby following birth. However, each year a significant number of babies are born with serious abnormalities of their kidneys which will result in total failure of kidney function and thus the need for dialysis treatment and a kidney transplant.

Urine infection may affect up to one in five children and for many will be responsible for causing kidney failure and high blood pressure. Recurrent infection is probably still responsible for the largest number of patients accepted onto national dialysis and kidney transplant programmes by the time children and adolescents reach adulthood.

Research into the cause of congenital defects of the kidney and the prevention of long term kidney disease are essential in order to reduce the effect of this chronic disease in childhood.

Richard Trompeter

Dr Richard S Trompeter MB FRCP
Consultant Paediatrician & Paediatric Nephrologist at Great Ormond Street Hospital For Children.

Contents

Starters

Anton Mosimann
Tomato, Mozzarella & Basil Terrine

Anne Robinson
Napa Valley Pasta

Jeremy Clarkson
Cucumber Mousse

Antony Worrall Thompson
Grilled Scallops with Avocado-Corn
Relish on Crispy Tortilla

John Major
Tuna Mousse

Lennox Lewis
Pepperpot Soup

Fiona Phillips
Broad Bean & Thyme Risotto

Jane Asher
Iced Avocado Soup

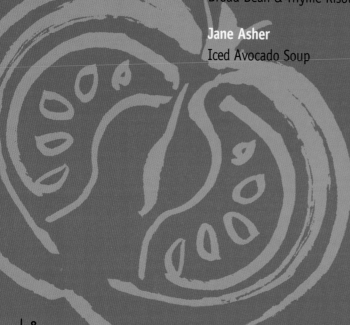

Anton Mosimann

Tomato, Mozzarella & Basil Terrine

Method:

Serves 4

1 Cut the tomatoes to fit a small, deep terrine dish. Hold a tomato upright, stem uppermost, and cut down thick slices off the four sides, leaving a square core in the middle (discard this). This will give you four roughly rectangular 1.5 cm (½ inch) thick slices. Cut all the tomatoes similarly. Flatten the slices gently under the palm of your hand and trim into neat rectangles.

2 Cut the mozzarella into similar slices, and trim into neat rectangles.

3 Wash the basil, gently pat dry, and pick off the leaves. Line the terrine with cling film.
Place a layer of sliced tomatoes, skin side down, into the base of the terrine. Try to make the slices fit exactly to give a neat final effect. Season well and add a layer of mozzarella slices, followed by a layer of basil leaves. Keep adding layers in the same order, finishing with a layer of tomato.
Cover with cling film and a flat piece of card cut to fit the top of the terrine exactly. Place a light weight on top and chill for several hours. This will help the layers stick together.
To serve, unmould carefully on to a chopping board, and slice into thick individual slices.

4 Garnish each plate with a sprig of basil and drizzle with olive oil and balsamic vinegar.

Ingredients:

12-14 large ripe plum tomatoes

500g (18oz) mozzarella cheese

large bunch fresh basil

salt and freshly ground pepper

4 sprigs fresh basil

good olive oil and balsamic vinegar

Anne Robinson

Napa Valley Pasta

Ingredients:

450g (1lb) plum tomatoes

1 red pepper

1 yellow pepper

100g (4oz) asparagus tips

175g (6oz) courgettes

1 head fennel

225g (8oz) red onions

6 cloves garlic, peeled

30ml (2 tablespoons) olive oil

salt and freshly ground black pepper

350g (12oz) fresh tagliatelle

Extra Virgin olive oil and fresh basil leaves to taste

Method:

Serves 4

I created this wonderfully fresh pasta dish while holidaying in the Napa Valley, California. It works well as a starter or a main course. Fresh vegetables and fresh pasta are the essential ingredients. Choose the vegetables according to your own taste.

1 Peel, core and slice the plum tomatoes. Deseed and slice the peppers, trim the asparagus and slice the remaining vegetables into strips. Leave cloves of garlic whole and arrange in a lightly oiled shallow, rimmed baking tray. Brush with more oil and season with salt and pepper. Bake in the oven at 200°C, 400°F, Gas Mark 6. Remove the asparagus tips after five minutes and keep warm. Stir the remaining vegetables about then continue to roast them for a further fifteen minutes.

2 Cook the fresh tagliatelle, drain and place on a serving plate. Place the roasted vegetables on top of the pasta. Add Extra Virgin olive oil and fresh basil leaves to taste. Bring to the table and stir prior to serving.

Jeremy Clarkson

Cucumber Mousse

Ingredients:

1 large cucumber

175g (6oz) curd/cream cheese

1 teaspoon onion juice

15g (½oz) gelatine soaked in 3 tablespoons cold water

150ml (¼ pint) vegetable/chicken stock

2 tablespoons white wine vinegar

1 tablespoon caster sugar

pinch ground mace/coriander

150ml (¼ pint) double cream, whipped until it forms thin ribbons

1 litre (1½-2 pint) capacity ring mould

vegetable oil

salt and pepper

prawns, watercress and/ or green peppers to garnish

Method:

Serves 6

1 Oil the ring mould.
Peel and dice the cucumber finely, sprinkle with salt and press between two plates for 30 minutes.
Sprinkle the gelatine over cold water and leave until spongy.
Grate the onion and mix the juice with the cheese and seasoning.
Whip the cream and put it in the fridge.
Pour boiling stock over the gelatine and stir until dissolved.
Leave to cool.
Drain the cucumber. Mix it with the vinegar, sugar and spices.
Add the gelatine to the cheese mix. Add the cucumber.
Lastly, fold in the cream.
Pour into the mould and leave overnight. Bring to room temperature 1 hour before turning out.

2 Fill the centre of the ring with prawns and garnish with watercress or green pepper slices.

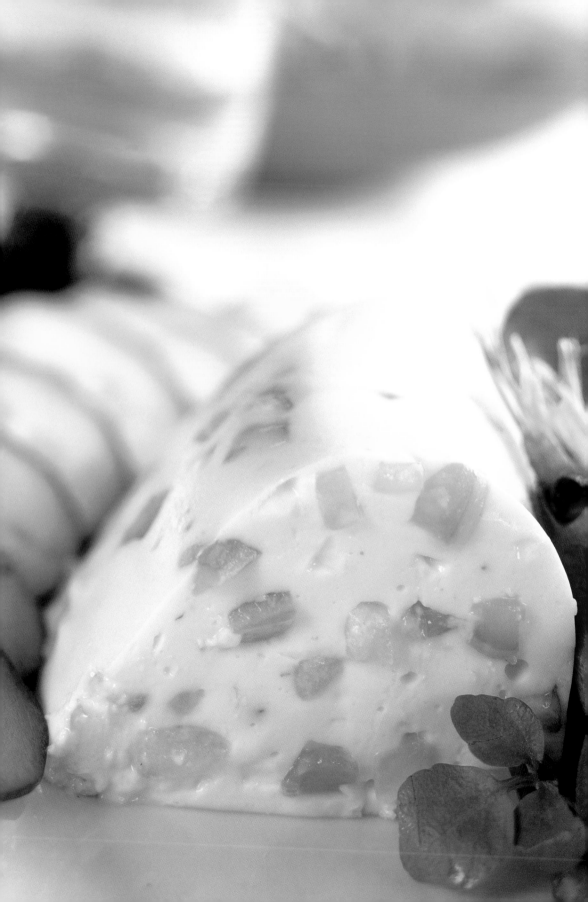

Antony Worrall Thompson

Grilled Scallops, Avocado-Corn Relish on Crispy Tortilla

Method:

Serves 4

1 Combine all the Avocado-Corn Relish ingredients. Do not place in a food processor. **IT SHOULD BE CHUNKY.**
Season to taste.

2 Rip each tortilla into five jagged pieces. Do not cut in neat triangles.
Fry in hot corn oil until golden and crispy, then drain on kitchen paper. Season and set aside in an airtight plastic container until ready for use.

3 Cook the scallops in butter for 30 seconds each side just prior to serving.

4 Blanch the coriander leaves in boiling water for 30 seconds and refresh in iced cold water. Squeeze dry. Blend the leaves and extra virgin olive oil together in a food processor and put in a bottle. Shake well before use.

Presentation:

Arrange four teaspoons of Avocado-Corn Relish on each of the four plates. Place four pieces of tortilla on each dollop of relish. Place another teaspoon of relish on top of each tortilla wedge, then top with the halves of grilled scallop. Season. Dribble with the coriander oil.

Ingredients:

AVOCADO-CORN RELISH:

2 haas avocados, peeled, seeded and mashed

1 corn-on-the-cob, blanched, chargrilled and nibs removed

1 chilli, finely diced

½ teaspoon coriander powder

½ teaspoon cumin powder

½ small red onion, finely diced

2 plum tomatoes, seeded and diced

½ bunch coriander, leaves only finely chopped

juice of 1 lime

2 tablespoons good olive oil

salt and ground black pepper

TORTILLA:

1 packet supermarket bought flour tortillas

150ml (¼ pint) corn oil

salt and ground black pepper

SCALLOPS:

2 large diver-caught scallops per person, cut in two horizontally

CORIANDER OIL:

2 bunches coriander, leaves only

600ml (1 pint) extra virgin olive oil

John Major

Tuna Mousse

Ingredients:

185g (6½ oz) can tuna in brine, drained

2 tablespoons low oil mayonnaise

2 tablespoons lemon juice

1 small onion, finely chopped

1 gherkin, finely chopped

1 tablespoon chopped fresh parsley

1 tablespoon tomato paste

½ teaspoon dry mustard

¼ teaspoon sugar

3 teaspoons gelatine

2 tablespoons water

Method:

Serves 4

1 Blend or process the tuna, mayonnaise, lemon juice, onion and gherkin until smooth. Add the parsley, tomato paste, mustard and sugar, and process until combined. Sprinkle the gelatine over water, and dissolve over hot water (or microwave on HIGH for about 20 seconds). Stir into tuna mixture.

2 Rinse 4 individual half cup capacity dishes; do not dry them. Divide the mixture evenly between the dishes; cover and refrigerate for several hours or overnight.

Lennox Lewis

Pepperpot Soup

Ingredients:

1kg (2lb) lean stewing beef

1.8 litres (3 pints) water

500g (1lb) kale, chopped

500g (1lb) callaloo or spinach leaves, washed and chopped

1 onion, chopped

2 green peppers, seeded and chopped

2 spring onions chopped

250g (8oz) sweet potatoes, peeled and sliced

1 large potato, sliced

1 sprig thyme

1 garlic clove, crushed

24 okras, trimmed and sliced

25g (1oz) butter

150ml (¼ pint) coconut milk

salt and freshly ground black pepper

FOR THE 'DUMPLINS':

250g (8oz) flour

pinch salt

2 teaspoons baking powder

25g (1oz) margarine

Method:

Serves 6

1 Trim any fat from the beef and cut the meat into cubes. Place in a large saucepan with the water and bring to the boil. Reduce the heat, cover the pan and simmer gently for 45 minutes.

2 Add the kale, callaloo or spinach leaves, onion, green peppers, spring onions, sweet potato, potato, thyme and garlic. Simmer gently in the covered pan for 15-30 minutes, until the vegetables are tender and the meat is cooked.

3 While the soup is cooking, make the 'dumplins'. Sift the flour, salt and baking powder into a bowl and rub in the margarine. Add sufficient water to mix a stiff dough. Knead until soft and smooth and shape into 18 balls. Flatten them and cook in salted boiling water for 10 minutes.

4 In a frying pan, fry the okra in the butter until golden brown on both sides. Remove and drain. Add to the soup with the coconut milk and simmer for 5 minutes. Season to taste and serve in individual bowls with the hot 'dumplins'.

Fiona Phillips

Broad Bean and Thyme Risotto

Ingredients:

350g (12oz) young broad beans shelled (1 kg (2lb 4oz) in their pods)

1 litre (1¾ pints) light vegetable stock

85g (3oz) unsalted butter

1 small onion, peeled and chopped

285g (10oz) risotto rice, Arborio or Carnaroli

150ml (5 fl oz) white wine

6 sprigs of thyme

60g (2oz) freshly grated Parmesan

FOR THE THYME CREAM:

2 heaped teaspoons chopped thyme

3 heaped dessertspoons crème fraîche

Method:

Serves 4

1 Bring a large pan of water to the boil and cook the beans (allow about 6 minutes for fresh ones). Cool under running water, skin and reserve them. Heat the stock to simmering point on the stove, and keep on a low heat while cooking the risotto.

2 Heat just over half of the butter in a heavy-bottomed pan and sweat the onion over a low heat until translucent and soft; it must not colour. Add the rice and cook for 1 to 2 minutes. Pour in the wine and continue to cook until the liquid has been absorbed. Add the thyme sprigs and start to pour in ladles of simmering stock - at no stage should the rice be flooded. It will take about 25 minutes to cook.

3 Stir in the Parmesan and the remaining butter. Remove the thyme sprigs and add the beans to heat through. Adjust seasoning and serve with a spoonful of thyme cream in the centre.

Jane Asher

Iced Avocado Soup

Ingredients:

2 ripe avocados

1 teaspoon chopped chives
or minced onion

6 tablespoons lemon juice

750ml (1¼ pint) chicken stock

1 x 150g (5oz) carton natural
yoghurt

2 tablespoons single cream
or sour cream

salt and black pepper

Method:

Serves 6

This was one of the first starters I ever made - and I still think it's
one of the easiest and most successful. Make sure the avocados
are ripe or it will be tasteless - it's always safest to buy them
several days, even a week, in advance, if you can. This soup needs
to be made on the day as it will discolour. Remove the top layer
before serving. Serve it with pieces of crisp Melba toast.

1 Scoop the flesh from the avocados and blend it with the
chives (or onion) and the lemon juice until smooth. Add
the remaining ingredients, blend again and season to taste.
Transfer to a bowl, cover with cling film and chill in the fridge
until ready to serve.

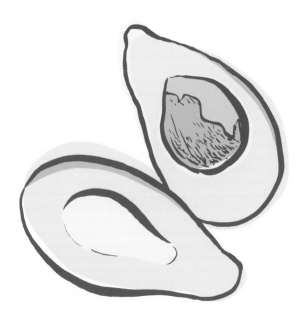

(See photograph on page 9)

Main Courses

Anthea Turner
Smoked Fish Pie

Kelly Brook
Lamb & Spinach Bhaji

Chris Eubank
Jamaican Lamb Curry

Emma Noble
Lamb Stew with
Coriander & Orange

Tony Blair
Ragout of Lamb
with Cous Cous

Sue Lawley
Spicy Chicken

Ian Woosnam
Woosie's Shepherds Pie

Delia Smith
Braised Lamb with
Flageolet Beans

Greg Turner
Butterflied leg of
Lamb Barbecued with
Indian Spices

Paul & Stacey Young
Penne Pomodoro

Imogen Stubbs
Fajitas

Aldo Zilli
Rack of Lamb with Rosemary

Terence Conran
Rump of Lamb with
Broad Beans & Basil Jus

Mark McCormack
Hot & Tangy Chicken

Fiona Fullerton
Bangkok Chicken & Rice

Peter Gordon
Citrus Lamb &
Chilli Casserole

Duchess of York
Noisettes of Lamb
with Redcurrant Sauce

Robson Green
Seafood Tagliatelle

Leslie Ash & Lee Chapman
Breakfast Mushrooms

Gary Lineker
Tofu Stir Fry

Barry Norman
Cous Cous with
Roasted Vegetables

Paddy Ashdown
Pasta with
two Cheeses

Vanessa Feltz
Sticky Chops

Michelle Collins
Beef Carbonade

Chris Tarrant
Hot Lamb Thai Salad

Simon Halliday
The Halliday
Chicken Recipe

Bruno Loubet
Lamb Neck Fillets
grilled with Mustard,
Honey & Pear

Greg Rusedski
Vegetable Lasagne

Frances & Phil Edmonds
Moussaka

Edwin Mullins
Moroccan Tajine with
Lamb & Potatoes

Anastasia Cooke
Cheesy Chicken & Broccoli

Anna Walker
Lamb Noisettes
with Spinach

Lorraine Kelly
Eezy Peezy Pizza

Anthea Turner

Smoked Fish Pie

Ingredients:

700g (1½ lb) smoked haddock

4 kipper fillets, weighing a total of 110-175g (4-6oz)

570ml (1 pint) milk

110g (4oz) butter

1 bay leaf

50g (2oz) flour

2 hard-boiled eggs, roughly chopped

3 tablespoons fresh chopped parsley

1 tablespoon capers (these can be left out if not available)

1 tablespoon lemon juice

salt and freshly milled black pepper

FOR THE TOPPING:

900g (2lb) fresh boiled potatoes

50g (2oz) butter

4 tablespoons milk

freshly grated nutmeg

25g (1oz) strong Cheddar cheese, grated

Method:

Serves 4

This is a lovely creamy fish pie with a mashed potato topping and a golden crust of melted cheese. You can in fact use any combination of smoked fish - sometimes a couple of ounces of smoked salmon offcuts make an interesting addition.

1 Pre heat the oven to 200°C, 400°F, Gas Mark 6.

2 Arrange the fish in a baking tin, pour half the milk over it, add a few flecks of the butter and the bay leaf, then bake in the oven for 15-20 minutes. Pour off and reserve the cooking liquid, then remove the skin from the fish and flake the flesh into largish pieces.

3 Next make the sauce by melting the remaining butter in a saucepan, then stirring in the flour and gradually adding the fish liquid bit by bit, stirring well after each addition. When all the liquid is in, finish the sauce by gradually adding the remaining milk, seasoning with salt and pepper and simmering for 3-4 minutes.

4 Now mix the fish into the sauce, together with the hard-boiled eggs, parsley and capers, then taste to see if it needs any more seasoning, and stir in the lemon juice. Pour the mixture into a buttered baking dish (about 1.5 litres (2½ pints) capacity).

5 Next prepare the topping. Cream the potatoes, starting off with a large fork, then finishing off with an electric beater if you have one, adding the butter and milk. Season the potatoes with salt and pepper and add some freshly grated nutmeg, spread evenly all over the fish then sprinkle the cheese all over. Bake on a high shelf in the oven - still at 200°C, 400°F, Gas Mark 6 for about 30 minutes, by which time the pie will be heated through and the top will be nicely tinged with brown.

Kelly Brook

Lamb & Spinach Bhaji

Ingredients:

500g (1lb) New Zealand Lamb neck fillet or leg meat, cut into thin strips

6 small cloves of garlic

2.5cm (1in) ginger, cut into match sticks

1 medium onion, sliced

5ml (1 teaspoon) cumin seeds

5ml (1 teaspoon) coriander seeds

5ml (1 teaspoon) caraway seeds

225g (8oz) ripe tomatoes, quartered

100g (4oz) cup mushrooms, quartered

100g (4oz) fresh spinach, prepared and roughly shredded

5ml (1 tablespoon) garam masala

Method:

Serves 4

1 Heat a wok or large frying pan. Mix the lamb with whole unpeeled garlic gloves, ginger, onion, cumin, coriander and caraway seeds.

2 Add this mixture to the pan and fry with no oil until the meat is sealed and starting to brown.

3 Add the tomatoes and mushrooms. Cook for another 5 minutes stirring occasionally.

4 Finally, mix in the spinach and sautée for 2 minutes until spinach is just cooked.

5 Sprinkle the garam masala on top and serve with naan bread.

Chris Eubank

Jamaican Lamb Curry

Ingredients:

900g (2lb) lamb steak or leg meat, cut into small pieces

1 onion, chopped

1 tomato, chopped

1 clove garlic, chopped

pinch thyme

1 large tablespoon curry powder

Method:

Rub the curry powder well into the meat. Heat a small amount of oil in a large pan and turn down low so that you can 'ardly see the flame. Add the meat and the other ingredients. The mixture will produce its own juice and will cook in just over an hour.

Enjoy your meal!

Emma Noble

Lamb Stew with Coriander & Orange

Ingredients:

500g (1lb 2oz) boned shoulder of lamb

1 teaspoon plain flour

salt & freshly ground black pepper

2 teaspoons ground coriander

1 teaspoon cooking oil

1 medium onion, chopped

1 clove garlic, crushed

2 carrots, sliced

1 medium orange

420g (15oz) butter beans

chopped coriander for garnish

Method:

Serves 4

1 Trim any fat from the meat and cut it into small pieces. In a plastic bag mix the flour with salt, pepper and coriander, add the meat and shake until evenly coated.

2 Heat the oil in a pan. Add the onion, garlic and carrot and fry until brown. Add the meat and fry also until brown.

3 Scrub the orange rind then pare with a potato peeler. Chop three quarters of the peel and shred the remainder. Squeeze the juice from the orange and add to the pan with the chopped rind, butter beans and liquor.

4 Bring the stew to the boil then reduce the heat, cover and simmer for 45 minutes until the meat is tender.

5 Serve scattered with the orange rind strips and freshly chopped coriander.

(See photograph on page 25)

Tony Blair

Ragout of Lamb with Cous Cous

This is one of the chef's 'specials' at Chequers and a particular favourite of the children.

Method:

Serves 4

1 Fry the seasoned meat in the oil with the onion, garlic and green pepper.

2 Drain off any excess oil and add flour.

3 Cook out the flour gently and then gradually add the stock and juice from the tomatoes.

4 Cook for 15 minutes before adding the chopped tomato and mushrooms.

5 Cook until the meat is tender, check the seasoning and add coriander.

6 Serve with coriander flavoured cous cous and garden vegetables.

Ingredients:

500g (1lb 2oz) stewing lamb

100g (3½oz) onions

1 tin plum tomatoes

1 clove garlic

chopped coriander

1 green pepper

200g (7oz) button mushrooms

25g (1oz) flour

2 tablespoons olive oil

600ml (1 pint) brown stock

Sue Lawley RECIPE BY DAUGHTER HARRIET

Spicy Chicken

Ingredients:

1 small corn-fed, free range chicken

50g (2oz) butter

250g (8oz) mushrooms, chopped

450g (1lb) tomatoes, skinned

1 green chilli, deseeded and finely chopped

1 clove garlic, crushed

15ml (1 tablespoon) fresh basil, chopped

salt

pinch of sugar

225g (8oz) rice, easy cook

Method:

Serves 4

1 Smear the chicken with half the butter and roast in an ovenproof dish at 180°C, 350°F, Gas Mark 4 for about 50 minutes. Remove from dish, wrap in foil and keep warm.

2 Cook the mushrooms in remaining butter in a frying pan. Remove and keep warm.

3 Roughly blend together the tomatoes, chilli, garlic, basil, salt and sugar to make a salsa. Chill.

4 Cook the rice following packet instructions, drain and, at the last moment, tip it into the ovenproof dish in which you cooked the chicken. Add the mushrooms, and finally the juice which has drained from the chicken (inside and out). Mix thoroughly.

5 Serve on warm plates with salsa and a leafy, French-dressed salad. The mixture of hot and cold, spicy and herby, soft and crunchy is perfect.

Ian Woosnam

Woosie's Shepherds Pie

Ingredients:

900g (2lb) potatoes, mashed with milk, butter and seasoning

1 tablespoon virgin olive oil

1 large onion, chopped

450g (1lb) minced lamb

2 carrots, diced

60-80g (2-3oz) peas - if frozen cook beforehand

lamb stock

2 level teaspoons mixed herbs

2 tablespoons Worcestershire sauce (optional)

Bisto thickening

After a hard day on the golf course I like to come home to my favourite meal.

Method:

Serves 4

1 Heat the oil and add the chopped onions, fry for about 5 minutes.

2 Add the mince and continue to fry for about 8-10 minutes. Add the carrots and peas and mix together.

3 Add the stock along with the herbs and Worcestershire sauce if using. Simmer for 20 minutes then thicken with Bisto. Add seasoning to taste.

4 Put into an ovenproof dish and top with the mashed potatoes. Grate cheese over the top if using and place the dish in a hot oven until golden brown on top.

5 Serve either on its own or with a crunchy spring green cabbage.

Delia Smith

Braised Lamb with Flageolet Beans

Ingredients:

900g (2lb) lamb neck fillets

225g (8oz) flageolet beans

2 large onions, peeled, halved and cut into 1cm (½ inch) rounds

2 cloves garlic, finely chopped

25g (1oz) plain flour

1 dessertspoon chopped fresh thyme leaves

570ml (1 pint) supermarket lamb stock or water

3 small bay leaves

225g (8oz) cherry tomatoes

4 small fresh thyme sprigs

2 tablespoons oil

salt and freshly milled black pepper

Method:

Though neck fillet of lamb is quite an economical cut, it provides very sweet meat that responds perfectly to long slow cooking and if you add pre-soaked dried green flageolets to cook alongside it, these too absorb all the sweet flavours of the lamb, garlic and herbs, making this an extremely flavoursome and comforting winter warmer.

1 You will also need a flameproof casserole dish of approximately 2.25 litre (4 pint) capacity.

2 Pre-heat the oven to Gas Mark 1, 275°F (140°C)

3 You need to start this recipe off by soaking the beans. You can do this by covering the beans with twice their volume of cold water, then soaking them overnight. Alternatively, on the same day, boil them for 10 minutes then leave them to soak for a minimum of 2 hours.

4 When you're ready to cook the lamb, pre-heat the oven, trim off any really excess fat and then cut it into rounds about 2cm (¾ inch) thick. Now place the casserole over direct heat, add 1 tablespoon of oil then as soon as it's smoking hot, brown the pieces of meat, a few at a time, wiping them first with kitchen paper so that they're absolutely dry when they hit the fat (don't add more than 6 pieces at a time). Then as soon as each piece is nicely browned on both sides, remove the fillets to a plate and carry on until all the meat is browned. Next add the other tablespoon of oil and, keeping the heat high, brown the onions round the edges, moving them around until they take on a nice dark caramel colour - this will take about 5 minutes - then add the garlic, stir that into the onions and let it cook for another minute or so. Now sprinkle in the flour and give it all a good stir, allowing the flour to soak into the juices. Add thyme leaves, then gradually add the stock, stirring all the while as you pour it in. Next return the meat to the casserole and season it well with freshly milled black pepper, but no salt

at this stage. After that drain the beans, discarding their soaking water, and add them to the casserole as well. Finally add the thyme sprigs and bay leaves, and as soon as everything has come up to simmering point, place a tight-fitting lid on and transfer the casserole to the centre shelf of the oven. Give it 1½ hours and towards the end of that time pour boiling water over the tomatoes and then after 30 seconds drain off the water and slip the skins off. Add these to the casserole along with a good seasoning of salt, then replace the lid and carry on cooking for a further hour.

5 Before serving remove bay leaves and sprigs of thyme and taste to check the seasoning.

Greg Turner

Butterflied leg of Lamb Barbecued with Indian Spices

Ingredients:

1 boned leg of lamb

MARINADE:

300ml (½ pint) natural yoghurt

1 lemon, juice and grated rind

1 tablespoon tomato puree

3 cloves garlic, crushed

2.5cm (1in) freshly grated ginger

2 tablespoons sunflower oil

1 tablespoon ground coriander

1 tablespoon ground cumin

1 tablespoon ground garam masala

1 teaspoon ground turmeric

3 fresh chopped red chillies or

1 teaspoon chilli flakes
(more if you like it spicy)

1 teaspoon salt

MINT RAITA:

1 small carton natural yoghurt

handful of fresh mint, chopped

juice of a lemon

salt and pepper to taste

1cm (½ in) ginger, grated finely

1 clove garlic, crushed

Method:

1 Mix all the marinade ingredients together and marinade the lamb for several hours or overnight in the fridge.
Heat the barbecue until hot. Sear both sides of the lamb and cook on each side for about 20 minutes. If your barbecue has a hood, 15 minutes per side with the hood down. Allow to relax covered in foil for 15 minutes before carving.

2 Serve the lamb with Mint Raita (see below), Pilau Rice and a cucumber, tomato and red onion salad.

3 Mix together all the ingredients for the Mint Raita and keep chilled until ready to serve.

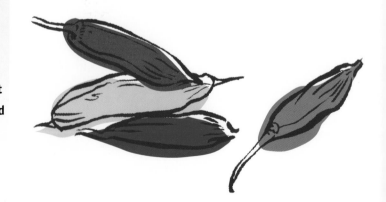

Paul & Stacey Young

Penne Pomodoro

Ingredients:

2 tablespoons olive oil

1 medium onion

1 clove garlic (optional)

2 x 14oz cans Italian plum tomatoes

1 sugar lump

salt & black pepper

1 cup Parmesan cheese

Method:

Serves 4

1 Heat the oil and gently fry first the garlic then the onion until soft but not brown.

2 Add the tinned tomatoes in juice, salt, sugar and black pepper and cook on a fairly high heat for about 20 minutes, stirring occasionally. If you don't have a blender, at this point you might want to chop the tomatoes with the spatula as you stir. Otherwise, when it's reduced and thick, blend it! Now you can add a 185g tin of drained tuna to the sauce and simmer it for another 10 minutes for a variation: Penne Tonno Pomodoro.

3 If you're a pro, you put enough penne for four into some lightly salted boiling water about ten minutes ago and that should be done too. Check it's just less than firm to the bite and you're done. After draining the pasta, add a little Parmesan to it before you add the sauce.

Imogen Stubbs RECIPE BY DAUGHTER ELLIE

Fajitas

Ingredients:

1 piece of chicken

1 onion

1 red pepper

1 green pepper

4 tortillas

1 small pot of sour cream

1 small pot of salsa

1 tablespoon olive oil

Method:

I would like to share with you one of my favourite recipes.
Ellie Nunn, aged 6¾.

1 Chop up the chicken, peppers, and onion into thin strips.
Heat the olive oil in a pan, add the chicken, peppers and
onion and stir fry all together until they are cooked.

2 Heat the tortillas in the oven until they are warm. Take 1
tortilla, and with a spoon spread on a little sour cream and
salsa, add some chicken, peppers and onion and roll it up with the
filling inside and eat it. *YUM YUM!*

Aldo Zilli

Rack of Lamb with Rosemary

Ingredients:

1.4kg (3lb) medium-sized baking potatoes, peeled and quartered

120ml (8 tablespoons) olive oil

900g (2lb) baby carrots with green fronds, most of green trimmed

8 baby aubergines

4 garlic cloves, lightly crushed

8 small racks of lamb, each with 4 cutlets

100g (4oz) dried breadcrumbs

2 sprigs of fresh rosemary, stalks removed and leaves chopped

30ml (2 tablespoons) chopped fresh flat-leaf parsley

30ml (2 tablespoons) chopped fresh sage

1 fresh red chilli, seeded and finely chopped

salt and freshly ground black pepper

30ml (2 tablespoons) smooth mustard

FOR THE GRAVY:

15ml (1 tablespoon) balsamic vinegar

150ml (5floz) red wine

150ml (5floz) vegetable stock

25g (1oz) butter

Method:

Serves 8

I do like using this particular cut of lamb for roasting, although if you are cooking for lots of people you might prefer to roast a whole leg. In my family, we would roast the whole lamb, with fresh hard herbs, such as bay leaf, and garlic.

1 Pre-heat the oven to 190°C, 375°F, Gas Mark 5. Bring a large pan of water to the boil. Add the potatoes and parboil for 5 minutes, then drain.

2 Place 60ml (4 tablespoons) of the oil in a large roasting tin and heat in the oven for 5 minutes until almost smoking. Quickly add the potatoes to the tin and shake about to coat with the hot oil. Add the carrots, aubergines and garlic. Roast for 15 minutes.

3 Meanwhile, heat the remaining oil in another roasting tin on top of the hob and sear the racks of lamb all over for 5-8 minutes. Turn the racks bone side down. Transfer the tin to the oven and roast the lamb for 10 minutes.

4 In a large bowl, mix together the breadcrumbs, herbs and chilli and season with salt and freshly ground black pepper.

5 Spread the mustard over the thin layer of fat on the tops of the racks of lamb and press the breadcrumb mixture on the mustard. Return to the oven and roast for a further 5 minutes until the lamb is cooked to your taste. Allow to rest while making the gravy.

6 Pour off and discard as much fat as possible from the roasting tin, then place it on the hob. Add the vinegar to the pan and deglaze, scraping all the bits of meat and sediment off the bottom. Stir in the red wine and stock and boil for 5 minutes until syrupy. Away from the heat whisk in the butter. Strain through a sieve. Season to taste with salt and freshly ground black pepper.

7 Serve the lamb with the vegetables and gravy.

Recipe reproduced by permission from 'Aldo's Italian Food for Friends' (published by Metro).

Terence Conran

Rump of Lamb with Broad Beans &

Ingredients:

4 x 170g (6oz) lamb rump
(trim off excess fat and internal
fat & sinew deposits)

10ml (1 dessertspoon) olive oil

salt & pepper

1 sprig thyme

½ teaspoon chopped rosemary
1 clove garlic (peeled & split
in two)

BEAN PUREE:

400g (14oz) broad beans
(blanched & outer skin removed)

200g (7oz) petit pois
(cooked & pureed)

1 sprig mint

20ml (2 dessertspoons) white
chicken stock

20g (¾oz) unsalted butter

30g (1¼oz) shallots (finely
chopped)

SAUCE & GARNISH:

12 banana shallots (roasted in
skins for 20 minutes, then skins
removed)

1/4 litre (9floz) lamb stock

100g (3½oz) chopped tomatoes

5 large basil leaves (chopped)

25g (1oz) butter (cold)

Method:

1 Place the oil into a sauté pan and heat through. Add the garlic, thyme & rosemary.

2 Seal the lamb in the hot oil on both sides for 2 minutes.

3 Place into a very hot oven 200-225°C, 400-440°F, Gas Mark 7 and roast for 8 minutes.

4 Prepare the bean and puree mixture by cooking the shallots in the butter for a couple of minutes. Add the puree of petit pois, the mint and the beans. Add the chicken stock and bring to the boil. Remove from the heat and keep warm on the side.

5 Warm the roast shallots through in the oven.

6 Remove meat from the oven and allow to rest on a plate for 3-5 minutes before carving - this is an option; you can leave the meat whole if you like.

7 Warm the sauce through, reduce a little. Then, away from the flame, add the cold

butter, the basil and tomato. Whisk it until it has incorporated into the sauce.

8 Take 4 large plates and place 3 shallots at the top of each one. Place a spoonful of the puree next to the shallots, arrange the rump of lamb next to the puree and spoon the sauce over the lamb and plate. Alternatively you can carve the lamb if you desire.

9 **Lamb stock:**
(approximate yield
2 litres/3½ pints)
1kg (2lb 4oz) lamb bones
(chopped)
500g (1lb 2oz) chopped onion,
carrot, celery, leek
100g (3½oz) tomato paste
3 cloves garlic (crushed)
1 x 250g (9oz) tin plum
tomatoes
1 sprig rosemary
1 sprig thyme
1 sprig tarragon
½ sprig marjoram
1 bay leaf
½ litre (18floz) white chicken
stock
2½ litres (4½ pints) water
20ml (2 dessertspoons) olive oil

Basil Jus

Serves 4

Roast the lamb bones until golden brown, then drain off excess fat.

10 Place the roasting pan onto a flame, add the chicken stock and bring to the boil. Remove from heat.

11 In a saucepan, heat the olive oil and add the vegetables to the pan in the order they are listed, allowing a couple of minutes cooking time between each vegetable.

12 Add the tomato paste and herbs. Cook out for 2-3 minutes.

13 Add the plum tomatoes, water and contents of the roasting pan.

14 Bring to the boil, skimming excess grease off the top of the stock. Allow to simmer for 2-3 hours.

15 Remove from the heat and pass off through a fine strainer.

Mark McCormack

Hot & Tangy Chicken

Ingredients:

2 chicken breast halves, skinned & boned

2 tablespoons cornflour

1 tablespoon dry sherry or water

1 large clove garlic, minced

225ml (8floz) reduced-salt chicken stock

4 teaspoons distilled white vinegar

½ teaspoon crushed red pepper

2 tablespoons vegetable oil

2 carrots, cut into julienne strips

2 large green peppers, cut into julienne strips

3 tablespoons light soy sauce

hot cooked pasta or rice

Method:

Serves 4

1 Cut the chicken into thin strips, and mix with 1 tablespoon of the cornflour, the sherry and garlic. Let it stand for 10 minutes.

2 Combine the next 3 ingredients with the remaining cornflour and set aside. Heat 1 tablespoon of the oil in a wok or large skillet over a medium high heat. Add the chicken and stir fry for 3 minutes, then remove from the skillet. Heat the remaining oil in the same pan over a high heat. Add the vegetables, and stir fry for 2 minutes. Return the chicken to the pan with stock mixture. Cook, stirring until the sauce boils and thickens. Remove from the heat, and stir in soy sauce. Serve immediately over pasta or rice.

Fiona Fullerton

Bangkok Chicken & Rice

Method:

Serves 6-8

1 In spite of its name, this is one of the great dishes from the famous Indonesian Rijstafel. It makes an attractive centrepiece for a buffet, surrounded by small dishes of colourful fresh vegetables and fruit to which guests help themselves.

2 Put the chicken in a large pan, with one whole peeled onion, the bay leaf and parsley sprig. Add a seasoning of salt and freshly ground pepper and enough cold water to cover the chicken. Bring to the boil, remove any scum from the surface, then cover the pan with a lid and simmer over gentle heat for about 2 hours or until the chicken is tender.

3 Lift out the chicken and leave to cool slightly. Strain the stock through a fine sieve and use it to cook the rice until just tender. Drain the rice through a colander and cover it with a dry cloth.

4 Remove the skin from the

chicken and cut the meat into small pieces. Peel and thinly slice the remaining onions. Heat the oil in a large pan, and fry the onions over low heat until they begin to colour. Stir in the peanut butter and chilli powder. Add the peeled prawns, diced ham and the chicken and finally the rice, which should now be dry and fluffy. Continue frying over low heat, stirring frequently until the rice is slightly brown. Crush the cumin and coriander seeds and the peeled garlic, and stir them, with the mace, into the rice. Season to taste with salt. Pile the rice and chicken mixture on to a hot serving dish and garnish with thin slices of unpeeled cucumber, wedges of hardboiled egg and large prawns.

Ingredients:

1 small boiling chicken (approx. 1.6kg/3½ lb)

450g (1lb) onions

1 bay leaf

1 sprig parsley

salt and black pepper

450g (1lb) long grain rice

3 tablespoons olive or vegetable oil

2 level tablespoons peanut butter

½ level teaspoon chilli powder

110g (4oz) peeled prawns

110g (4oz) diced cooked ham

1 level teaspoon cumin seeds

1½ level teaspoons coriander seeds

1 clove garlic

pinch ground mace

GARNISH:

half a cucumber

2 hardboiled eggs

8-12 unpeeled prawns

Recipe printed with the permission of Reader's Digest Association Ltd - 'Reader's Digest Cookery Year', 1973 and 1988.

Peter Gordon

Citrus Lamb & Chilli Casserole

Ingredients:

1 leg of lamb, boned and trimmed of excess fat, cut into 8 chunks

50ml (2floz) olive oil

3 red onions, peeled and thickly sliced

8 cloves of garlic, unpeeled

1 x 6cm (2½in) piece of fresh rosemary, leaves removed

2 red chillies, finely sliced into rings

2 stems of celery, cut into ½cm (¼in) pieces

1 parsnip, peeled and cut into ½cm (¼in) dice

1 teaspoon cumin seeds (optional)

30ml (1floz) vinegar

50ml (2floz) soy sauce

1 orange

3 tablespoons chopped fresh mint

3 tablespoons chopped parsley

Method:

Serves 6-8

1 Pre-heat the oven to 170°C, 325°F, Gas Mark 3. Heat the oil in a pan and add the onions, garlic, rosemary, chillies, celery and parsnips (and cumin if using). Stir occasionally and cook over moderate heat until the onions are browned.

2 Remove the onions mixture from the pan, but keep most of the oil still in the pan. Heat the oil up again then place the lamb chunks in one layer in the pan and brown on all sides. You may have to cook it in two batches.

3 Return the onion mixture to the pan and add the vinegar and soy, then add enough hot water to almost cover the meat.

4 Using a sharp knife or potato peeler, peel the rind off the orange in strips, then juice the orange, and add the juice and peel to the pan. Bring to a rapid simmer on top of the stove, then seal the pan with foil and place in the oven.

5 Cook for 1½ to 2 hours, at which point the lamb should be tender. Check for seasoning, then stir in the chopped mint and parsley and serve. This dish is delicious served with mashed potatoes.

Duchess of York

Noisettes of Lamb with Redcurrant Sauce

Serves 4

Method:

1 Pan fry the fillets using a small amount of olive oil in a heavy based pan. This should be for around 4 minutes, turning occasionally so all sides are browned. The meat should be pink in the middle.

2 Remove from the pan and cut into noisettes, arranging them on a serving dish and put in the oven or warmer while you prepare the redcurrant sauce.

3 Using the juices from the pan, add the flour, and a little water or lamb stock. Making sure that the flour is well mixed in, add a little red wine and the redcurrants. Simmer gently until the redcurrants are soft and add the salt and pepper to taste.

4 Pour the sauce over the lamb and garnish with a few fresh redcurrants and a sprig of mint.

5 Serve with new potatoes and vegetable of your choice or green salad.

Ingredients:

2 fillets of lamb

110g (4oz) fresh redcurrants

1 tablespoon flour

4 tablespoons lamb stock or water

4 tablespoons red wine

freshly ground salt and pepper

Robson Green

Seafood Tagliatelle

Ingredients:

400g (1 pint) prawns, peeled

450g (1lb) cod

450g (1lb) salmon

2 tablespoons vegetable oil

2 cloves of garlic, crushed

1 medium onion

3 tablespoons cornflour
to thicken

425ml (¾ pint) milk

120g (¼ lb) Cheddar
cheese, or however
much you like (to taste)

4 tablespoons dry white wine

1lb fresh tagliatelle

Method:

1 Fry the garlic and onion in oil and wine for about
2 minutes. Add cornflour to make a roux. Add milk and
simmer until it thickens.

2 Add the seafood and cook for 2 minutes on a low heat.

3 At the same time cook fresh tagliatelle in a pan of salted
water for 3-4 minutes.

4 Drain the pasta, add to seafood and enjoy!

Picture Courtesy of Dave Hogan, All Action Pictures

Leslie Ash & Lee Chapman

Breakfast Mushrooms

Ingredients:

4 large cup mushrooms

1 smoked kipper, filleted

3 rashers bacon

1 tomato

1 small onion

1 clove garlic

Swiss cheese

Method:

1 Stalk the mushrooms (keep the stalks).

2 Chop the stalks, kipper, bacon, tomato, onion, garlic and fry all together until cooked.

3 Then spoon the mixture into the mushrooms and top with grated cheese.

4 Place under medium grill and heat until cheese starts to melt.
Serve with toast.

Gary Lineker

Tofu Stir Fry

Ingredients:

2 tablespoons olive oil

250g (1 pack) fresh tofu

1 courgette, sliced

100g (1 small bag) beansprouts

6 baby corn on the cob, each cut into 3 pieces

8 baby asparagus spears, left whole

8 button mushrooms, cut into slices

2 tablespoons soy sauce

1 tablespoon chopped spring onion

2 teaspoons minced ginger root

150ml (¼ pint) vegetable stock

1 tablespoon sesame oil

Method:

Serves 4

This is one of my children's favourite dishes. They are not particularly bothered that it is very good for them - their only concern is that it tastes great!

1 Combine the soy sauce, spring onion, ginger, stock and sesame oil in a bowl.

2 Cut the tofu into strips 1cm (¼ in) x 1cm (¼ in) x 5cm (2in) and drain thoroughly.

3 Put the olive oil into a wok and heat until smoking. Add the tofu to the olive oil and fry until golden brown. Remove from the wok and drain well. Add all the vegetables (except the beansprouts) to the wok and fry for five minutes. Add the beansprouts, tofu and remaining ingredients, bring to the boil and simmer for two minutes.

4 Serve immediately with plain boiled rice.

Barry Norman
RECIPE BY DAUGHTER SAMANTHA

Cous Cous with Roasted Vegetables

Method: Serves 4

This is a family favourite, my father's take on a Delia Smith recipe, and enjoyed by absolutely everybody bar my mother who, for some inexplicable reason, hates cous cous. By the way, it's absolutely delicious with lamb.

1 Place the cous cous in a large bowl and pour over just enough boiling water to cover. Stir like mad until the cous cous has cooled. Add the lemon juice.

2 Place the chopped vegetables onto a large baking tray in a hot oven. Sprinkle (the vegetables, not the oven) with the chopped fresh basil, salt and olive oil.

3 Bake at 220°C, 425°F, Gas Mark 7 for 20-30 minutes (or until the vegetables are well-baked) and then add to the cous cous. Serve.

Ingredients:

1 x 250g (8oz) packet quick cook cous cous

juice of 2 lemons

3 peppers, any colour, deseeded and chopped

3 large tomatoes, chopped

1 medium aubergine, chopped

2 medium courgettes, chopped

2-3 tablespoons chopped fresh basil

sea salt

3-4 tablespoons olive oil

Paddy Ashdown

Pasta with two Cheeses

Ingredients:

1 large tin (400g/15oz) plum tomatoes

1 clove garlic, chopped

1 tablespoon olive oil (any oil will do)

2 teaspoons dried basil or five fresh basil leaves

50g (2oz) mature Cheddar cheese, grated

125g (5oz) packet mozzarella cheese, chopped into cubes

Any sort of pasta!

Method:

Serves 2

1 Put a large pan of slightly salted water on to boil.

2 In a heavy-based pan, mash the tomatoes with the back of a wooden spoon, add the oil, basil and garlic, and simmer gently so that the sauce thickens.

3 When the water boils, add the pasta, following the cooking instructions on the pack. It normally takes 10 minutes for pasta to be ready.

4 Now add the two cheeses to the tomato sauce, turning the heat right down. Stir well once, then leave while the pasta finishes off. If the sauce starts to stick, turn off the heat and cover with a lid to keep it hot.

5 Drain the pasta, turn into a serving dish and top with the sauce. Serve with a salad.

Picture Courtesy of Alan Davidson, All Action Pictures

Vanessa Feltz

Sticky Chops

Ingredients:

6 large chump chops

FOR THE SAUCE:

6 tablespoons tomato ketchup

3 tablespoons Worcestershire sauce

3 tablespoons runny honey

1 tablespoon soy sauce

1 teaspoon mustard

TO FINISH:

demerara sugar

Method:

1 Arrange the chops in an ovenproof dish.

2 Mix together the sauce ingredients and pour over the chops. Sprinkle demerara sugar over the whole thing and bake in the oven at 160°C, 320°F, Gas Mark 3 for 1 hour.

Michelle Collins

Beef Carbonade

Ingredients:

700g (1½ lb) chuck steak

2 tablespoons dripping

2 large onions, sliced

1 tablespoon flour

1 clove garlic, crushed

300ml (½ pint) brown ale

300ml (½ pint) hot water

bouquet garni

salt & pepper

1 teaspoon wine vinegar

pinch of sugar & nutmeg

Method:

Serves 4

1 Pre-heat the oven to 140°C, 275°F, Gas Mark 1. Heat the dripping in a frying pan until sizzling hot and add a few pieces of the chuck steak (cut into 5cm (2in) squares) at a time to brown. Once brown, remove the steak to a casserole dish. Now fry the onions and once cooked, add the flour and turn the heat down.

2 Mix in the garlic then gradually add the brown ale and bring the liquid to simmering point. Finally add the remaining ingredients and transfer to the casserole dish. Put a tight fitting lid on the dish and cook for 2½ hours.

Chris Tarrant

Hot Lamb Thai Salad

Method:

Serves 4

1 Toss all the salad ingredients together and turn into a serving dish.

2 Dry fry the lamb briskly until it is just cooked. Season with salt and freshly ground black pepper, then pile on top of the salad. Mix the dressing ingredients together.

3 Turn the mixture into the frying pan and swirl it around so it heats up and dissolves the frying residue.

4 Pour over the salad and serve immediately.

Ingredients:

450g (1lb) New Zealand lamb neck fillet or leg meat, cut into thin strips

½ Chinese lettuce, washed and shredded

¼ cucumber, thinly sliced

1 red onion, thinly sliced

10 radishes, thinly sliced

1 beefsteak tomato, cut into wedges

15ml (1 tablespoon) mint leaves, roughly chopped

15ml (1 tablespoon) coriander leaves, roughly chopped

15ml (1 tablespoon) basil leaves, roughly chopped

30ml (2 tablespoons) lime juice

30ml (2 tablespoons) light soy sauce

10ml (2 teaspoons) clear honey

3 cloves garlic, crushed

30ml (2 tablespoons) fresh ginger, coarsely grated

5ml (1 teaspoon) ground cumin

pinch of cayenne pepper

Simon Halliday

The Halliday Chicken Recipe

Ingredients:

225g (8oz) frozen or fresh broccoli, cut into florets

4 chicken breasts (skinned, cut into cubes)

4 tablespoons double cream

4 tablespoons mayonnaise

1 tin condensed chicken soup

½ teaspoon curry powder (medium hot)

Cheddar cheese (grated)

coriander (fresh)

2 cloves crushed garlic

Bag of ready salted crisps (crushed)

Method:

Serves 4

1 Place the broccoli, spread out, in a casserole dish. Next place the uncooked chicken on top. In a bowl mix together the cream, garlic, mayonnaise, coriander, condensed soup and curry powder. Pour the above mixture over the chicken, sprinkle with cheese and the crushed crisps, and bake at 200°C, 400°F, Gas Mark 6 for 40 minutes.

2 Serve with baby new carrots and new potatoes.

Bruno Loubet

Lamb Neck Fillets grilled with Mustard, Honey & Pear

Ingredients:

4 x 160g (5½ oz) neck fillet

2 tablespoons Meaux mustard

2 tablespoons honey

2 pears, halved

1 tablespoon grated Parmesan

1 tablespoon chopped basil

3 tablespoons olive oil

1 tablespoon balsamic vinegar

salt and pepper

Method:

Serves 4

1 Brush the pear halves with honey on both sides. Put on the barbecue. Open the fillet "butterfly", grill quickly on both sides, then brush with honey and mustard. Finish the cooking.

2 Place the lamb and pear on plates, sprinkle with Parmesan and basil, pour on some olive oil and balsamic vinegar and season. Serve with a green salad.

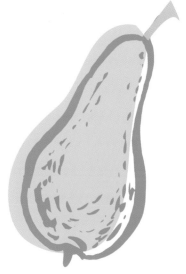

Greg Rusedski

Vegetable Lasagne

Ingredients:

10-12 strips lasagne

2 onions, peeled and finely chopped

2 tablespoons oil

1 clove garlic, crushed

350g (¾ lb) mushrooms, wiped and sliced

350g (¾ lb) courgettes, washed and sliced

3 teaspoons dried oregano

450g (1lb) tomatoes, skinned and chopped

1 tablespoon tomato puree

salt and freshly ground black pepper

Sauce

50g (2oz) butter

2 dessertspoons flour

600ml (1 pint) milk or single cream

4-6 tablespoons double cream (optional)

75-100g (3-4oz) Parmesan cheese, grated

Method:

Serves 4-6

1 Pre-heat the oven to 180°C, 350°F, Gas Mark 4. First cook the lasagne in boiling salted water (with a little oil added) for about 8-10 minutes. Drain and rinse in cold water. Gently fry the finely chopped onion in the oil for a few minutes and add the garlic. Add the sliced mushrooms and courgettes and fry these for a few minutes to seal in the flavour. Add the oregano, tomatoes and tomato puree. Cover the pan and cool for 10-15 minutes so that the flavours have a chance to blend. Season to taste.

2 Meanwhile, prepare the sauce. Melt the butter in a small saucepan and stir in the flour. Cook the roux for 2-3 minutes, then pour over the milk. Bring it to the boil, stirring constantly and cook for 5 minutes over a gentle heat. Then add the cream and cook gently for another minute.

3 Lightly grease a 2.3 litre (4 pint) ovenproof dish and put in a layer of vegetable sauce. Cover with lasagne and then a layer of cream sauce. Repeat these layers, ending with a layer of the cream sauce. Cover with grated cheese and bake for 35-40 minutes, when the cheese should be bubbling and golden. Serve immediately.

Frances & Phil Edmonds

Moussaka

Method:

1 Cut the aubergines into ½ cm/¼ inch thick slices. Sprinkle with salt and leave for 30 minutes. Drain thoroughly. Fry quickly in butter and oil until golden on both sides. Remove from the pan and leave on one side.

2 Slice onions thinly. Fry in remaining butter and oil until pale gold. Remove from heat.

3 Combine the lamb with breadcrumbs, water and tomato puree. Season to taste.

4 Line the base of an oblong or square heatproof dish with half the fried aubergine slices. Cover with lamb mixture and onions. Arrange the remaining aubergine slices attractively on top.

5 Gradually beat the egg into the cheese sauce (see below). Pour into the dish over the aubergine slices. Sprinkle with cheese. Bake, uncovered, in the centre of a moderate oven (180°C, 350°F, Gas Mark 4) for 45 minutes to one hour.

6 **Cheese Sauce:** Melt the butter in a pan. Add the flour and cook over a low heat, stirring for 2 minutes. Do not allow the mixture (roux) to brown.

7 Gradually blend in the milk. Cook, stirring, until the sauce comes to the boil and thickens.

8 Simmer very gently for 3 minutes.

9 Stir in the cheese, mustard and pinch of cayenne pepper. Season to taste with salt and pepper.

Serves 4

Ingredients:

2 medium sized aubergines

salt

75g (3oz) butter

1 tablespoon olive or corn oil

2 large onions

350g (12oz) cooked minced lamb

2 level tablespoons fresh white breadcrumbs

150ml (¼ pint) water

1 level tablespoon tomato puree

seasoning to taste

1 medium egg (beaten)

1 recipe freshly made cheese sauce (see below)

50g (2oz) grated Cheddar cheese

CHEESE SAUCE:

25g (1oz) butter

25g (1oz) flour

300ml (½ pint) milk

50g (2oz) finely grated Cheddar cheese

1 level teaspoon made mustard

pinch cayenne pepper

salt and pepper

Edwin Mullins

Moroccan Tajine with Lamb & Potatoes

Ingredients:

1.35kg (3lbs) boned lamb

1.35kg (3lbs) large waxy potatoes

1 large onion

1 (or more) teaspoonful saffron (the only expensive item)

80g (3oz) butter

1 handful fresh coriander

salt and black pepper

The family became used to me returning from distant places with strange local produce, often half-rotten by the time it was released by Customs. But when I staggered in carrying two huge earthenware cooking-pots with tall conical lids there was a cry of 'Oh God, what have you brought back this time, Dad?'

Moroccan cooking is some of the best in the world. Years before Robert Carrier brought out his splendid cookbook on the subject I got hold of a recipe-book somewhere in the labyrinthine bazaar in Fez, along with the earthenware pots - which are called tajines, hence the name of the dish. Here is one that doesn't require

Method:

unobtainable ingredients with unpronounceable names.

1 Chop the onion, melt the butter in a large casserole on the open stove, and cook until the onion turns colour. Then add the lamb chopped into 4-5cm (2in) cubes. Using a pestle and mortar pound the saffron finely in a little salt (to stop it smearing), and add most of it to the meat. Mix well. Everything will turn a lurid orange. Don't be alarmed. Cover with hot water, and when simmering cover and cook until the lamb is tender, stirring occasionally (about 1 hour). Add pepper to taste and check for salt.

2 Meanwhile scrub or peel the potatoes and chop into 3-5cm (1-2in) cubes. Heat the oven just high enough to keep things hot. Then roughly chop the coriander leaves.

3 When the lamb is tender transfer just the meat into the tajine, replacing its conical lid (which helps conserve heat and moisture), and place in the pre-heated oven. Add chopped potatoes to the casserole, mix

with the meat and onion juices, and stir in the remaining saffron and most of the coriander. Cover and cook until the potatoes are almost ready.

4 Then remove the lamb from the tajine and lay the pieces carefully on top of the potatoes in the casserole, and continue to cook gently for a further 5 minutes.

5 Finally return the lamb to the centre of the tajine and arrange the potatoes around it . Pour the juices over, and sprinkle with the rest of the coriander. Serve immediately, removing the lid of the tajine with a proud flourish. Serve with a salad or whatever green vegetables take your fancy. And a good red wine.

NB You no longer need to go to the bazaar in Fez in order to buy a tajine (though that may be more fun). There are firms that sell them in this country. Otherwise any ovenproof serving-dish will do, though less glamourously. And after all, a little glamour is part of the fun of cooking. Dads like to show off.

Serves 5

Anastasia Cooke

Cheesy Chicken & Broccoli

Ingredients:

2 chicken breasts, skinned

2 tablespoons vegetable oil or

300ml (½ pint) chicken stock

60g (2oz) pasta

65g (2¼ oz) broccoli, cut into small florets

450ml home made cheese sauce

pinch of mustard powder or nutmeg

1 egg yolk

Serves 4

Method:

1 Cut the chicken breasts into bite-sized pieces and either sauté in the vegetable oil or poach in the chicken stock until cooked through. Cook the pasta according to the instructions on the packet. Steam or boil the broccoli until tender and set aside.

2 When preparing the cheese sauce stir in the mustard or nutmeg. Mix together the chicken, broccoli, pasta and half the cheese sauce and place in an ovenproof dish. Beat the egg yolk into the rest of the cheese sauce and pour on top.

3 Bake in an oven preheated to 180°C, 350°F, Gas Mark 4 for 20 minutes and then brown the top under a grill.

Anna Walker

Lamb Noisettes with Spinach

Ingredients:

2 tablespoons olive oil

2 tablespoons mustard (honey or herb-flavoured)

8-12 lamb noisettes, about 800g (1lb 12oz) in total

2 large sprigs rosemary

salt and black pepper

½ red onion

3 cloves garlic

1 medium tomato

50g (1¾ oz) pine kernels

40g (1½ oz) seedless raisins

500g (1lb 2oz) young spinach

TO SERVE: crusty bread

Method:

Serves 4

1 Preheat the oven to 220°C, 425°F, Gas Mark 7. Use a little of the oil to grease a small baking tray.

2 Using half the mustard, spread some on top of each noisette. Rinse and dry the rosemary and snip some over the noisettes. Season with salt and pepper and set aside until the oven is hot enough. Peel and thinly slice the onion and garlic; rinse and chop the tomato. Set them aside.

3 Roast the noisettes on the top shelf of the oven for 10 minutes, then turn them over, spread with the remaining mustard, scatter with more rosemary, and season. Roast for another 5-8 minutes, until cooked but still slightly pink. If you prefer them well done, cook a few minutes longer.

4 While the lamb is cooking, heat the remaining oil in a large pan. Add the onion and garlic, cover and cook over a low heat for 5 minutes, or until the onion is soft but not coloured. Add the pine kernels and raisins and fry for 3 minutes.

5 Trim the spinach, then rinse and dry it thoroughly. Add the tomato to the pan and cook for 1 minute. Then add the spinach and a pinch of salt and stir for 3-4 minutes, until the spinach wilts and is only just cooked. If there is too much spinach to stir easily, cover the pan for a minute until the spinach wilts slightly, then uncover and stir-fry.

6 Divide the mixture among individual serving plates and arrange the lamb on top. Serve with crusty bread to mop up the juices.

Picture Courtesy of Doug Peters, All Action Pictures

Lorraine Kelly

Eezy Peezy Pizza

Method:

Serves 4

Making pizza has never been easier! Here's how to transform ready made pizza bases into something spectacular.

1 Preheat the oven to 200°C, 400°F, Gas Mark 6. Make up the pizza bases according to the instructions on the packet and place on a greased baking tray.

2 Simmer the tomatoes, tomato puree, onion and chilli powder together in a saucepan for 8-10 minutes until thick and reduced. Spread this tomato mixture over the pizza base (or, if using ready made tomato sauce, spread sauce from the jar over the pizza base). Scatter over the peppers and mushrooms and season well with salt and pepper. Sprinkle over the dried basil, the nuts and the Parmesan. Scatter over the Cheddar and olives. Drizzle over the 3 tablespoons of olive oil and bake for 15-20 minutes or until bubbling hot and golden brown. Serve at once.

Ingredients:

1 x 290g (10oz) packet pizza dough mix or 4 x 75g (3oz) ready made pizza bases.

FOR THE TOPPING:

400g (14oz) tin chopped tomatoes

1 tablespoon tomato puree

1 onion, finely chopped

1 teaspoon chilli powder

OR

1 jar ready made tomato sauce

AND

3 large red peppers, cut into thick strips

225g (8oz) large flat mushrooms, sliced

1½ tablespoons dried basil

75g (3oz) chopped almonds or any nuts

50g (2oz) Parmesan

50g (2oz) grated Cheddar cheese

12 pitted olives (optional)

3 tablespoons olive oil

salt and pepper

Desserts

Ronnie Corbett
Tarte Tatin

David Gower
Rhubarb Ice Cream

Zoe Ball
Lemon Cheesecake

Andy Mackay
Frozen Berries & White Chocolate Sauce

William Hague
Welsh Cakes

Jilly Goolden
Pip's Pudding

Raymond Blanc
Semoule Soufflée Aux Pommes

Michael Caine
Carrot Cake

Judi Dench
Bread & Butter Pudding

Ronnie Corbett

Tarte Tatin

Ingredients:

120g (4oz) unsalted butter

7 to 8 cooking apples (about 1.25kg or 2¾ lbs), preferably Jonathan or Granny Smith, peeled, quartered, and cored.

200g (7oz) sugar

Basic Pastry

210g (7oz) plain flour

105g (3½oz) unsalted butter, cubed at room temperature

1 tablespoon sugar

1 large egg

pinch of salt

1 tablespoon water approx.

A simple, foolproof Tarte Tatin recipe with well-caramelised apples and a layer of thin pastry. Golden Delicious apples could be used if necessary and although quite flavourless still produce a delicious tart when properly caramelised. The apples remain in large chunks, making for a rustic tart and the clear glass baking dish allows you to see if the apples are sticking as you turn out

Method:

the tart. Although this may seem like a lot of apples for a single tart, they cook down quickly.

1 **For the pastry:** Place the flour in a large shallow bowl and make a well in the centre. Add the butter, sugar, egg and salt to the well and mix them together with your fingers. Very gradually work in the flour. Sprinkle the water as needed over the flour mixture and knead until well blended. Wrap the pastry in plastic wrap and refrigerate for about 30 minutes. This makes enough pastry for one 27cm (10½ in) tart.

2 **For the tart:** Preheat the oven to 220°C, 425°F, Gas Mark 7. Melt the butter in a deep 30cm (12in) skillet over medium-high heat. Add the apples and sugar and stir to combine. Cook for 20 minutes, stirring carefully from time to time so the apples and sugar do not stick. Increase the heat to high and cook until the apples and sugar are a deep golden

brown, about 10 minutes longer. Watch carefully to be sure that the apples and sugar do not burn. (If you do not have a pan large enough to cook all of the apples, cook them in 2 smaller skillets, dividing the apples, butter and sugar evenly).

3 Literally pile the apples into an unbuttered round 27cm (10½ in) glass baking dish.

4 Roll out the dough slightly larger than the dish and place it on top of the apples, tucking a bit of the dough around the edge into the dish.

5 Bake until the apples bubble and the pastry is golden brown, about 20 minutes.

6 Remove the tart from the oven and immediately invert it onto a large heatproof serving platter. Serve warm or at room temperature.

David Gower

Rhubarb Ice Cream

Method:

Serves 4-6

Ingredients:

250g (8oz) rhubarb, trimmed and cut into 2.5cm (1in) chunks

125g (4oz) sugar

1 tablespoon water

250g (8oz) Greek yoghurt

2 egg whites

This recipe gets the stamp of approval from Alexandra (4½) and Samantha Gower (2).

1 Put the rhubarb, sugar and measured water in a large saucepan, cover and heat gently to simmering point. Remove the lid and cook gently for 10 minutes, by which time the rhubarb should have disintegrated to a mush.

2 Transfer the contents of the pan to a blender or food processor and process to a smooth purée. Scrape the purée into a large mixing bowl. Refrigerate until cool.

3 Add the yoghurt to the rhubarb purée, mixing well. Whisk the egg whites in a separate, grease-free bowl until stiff, then fold them into the rhubarb mixture. Pour the mixture into a suitable container for freezing.

4 Freeze the ice cream for several hours or until firm. There is no need to beat the ice cream during the freezing process, but it should be transferred to the refrigerator 20-30 minutes before serving so it is soft enough to be scooped into serving bowls.

(see photograph on page 4)

Picture Courtesy of Doug Peters, All Action Pictures
Recipe from 'Truly Wonderful Puddings and Desserts' by Susan Brooks, published by Hamlyn (a division of Octopus Publishing Group Limited).

Zoe Ball

Lemon Cheesecake

Ingredients:

60g (2oz) sugar

120g (4oz) digestive biscuits

90g (3oz) butter

75g (2½oz) caster sugar

350g (12oz) cottage cheese

2 large eggs

grated rind and juice of 2 lemons

15g (½ oz) powdered gelatine

150ml (5floz) double cream

Method:

Serves 4-6

1 **For the base:** Crush the digestives inside a polythene bag with a rolling pin. Melt the butter in a pan, add the sugar and biscuit crumbs, mix well and press into a buttered loose-bottomed cake tin or flan ring (20-22cm/8-9in).

2 **For the filling:** Put the gelatine with 3 tablespoons of cold water in a small bowl and dissolve over warm water. Put the egg yolks, sugar and cheese in a liquidiser, and blend for 1 minute. Add the lemon juice and rind plus the gelatine and blend until smooth. Whip the cream lightly and mix it with the cheese mixture. Pour this over the crumb base and leave it to set in the fridge. Decorate with frosted grapes or whipped cream.

Andy Mackay

Frozen Berries & White Chocolate Sauce

Method:

This is the simplest and most moreish pudding you will ever make and could become a dinner-party classic. My daughter Venice loves this 'pudding', it's very sweet.

1 Heat chocolate and condensed milk together over a low heat until blended. Arrange frozen fruits on decorative plate and pour over warm sauce. Serve immediately.

Ingredients:

Raspberries

Blueberries

Blackberries

Red, black, white currants

ALL THE ABOVE NEEDS TO BE IN THE FREEZER UNTIL FROZEN

FOR THE SAUCE:

200g white chocolate

½ can sweetened condensed milk

William Hague

Welsh Cakes

Ingredients:

225g (8oz) self-raising flour

110g (4oz) butter

110g (4oz) granulated sugar

60g (2oz) sultanas or currants

½ teaspoon cinnamon

1 beaten egg

pinch of salt

Method:

1 Sieve the flour, cinnamon and salt into a large bowl and add the butter. Rub together until the mixture resembles fine breadcrumbs. Add the sugar and mix well.

2 Wet the mixture with the beaten egg and knead it into a dough. Add the dried fruit and knead the dough again until the fruit is evenly distributed.

3 Roll out the dough on a floured surface and cut with a pastry cutter into small cakes. Cook the cakes on both sides over a low heat on a griddle or ungreased frying pan until they are golden brown. Delicious served warm or cold.

Picture Courtesy of Dave Benett

Jilly Goolden

Pip's Pudding

Ingredients:

2 cooking apples

a little sugar

bar of chocolate

Rice Krispies

Method:

My son Pip's choice of pudding would be anything with chocolate, as he is a confirmed choc-aholic. He also loves apples, so this simple pudding is a hit with him.

Peel, slice and cook the apples with the sugar and a bit of water in a covered pan. Melt the chocolate in a bowl over a pan of hot water. Add enough Rice Krispies to the chocolate for it all to stick together. Put the apples in the bottom of a shallow dish, and top with the chocolate Krispies. Chill in the fridge.

Raymond Blanc

Semoule Soufflée Aux Pommes
Apples baked in a Semolina Soufflé

Ingredients:

4 large ripe eating apples (James Greaves, Junagold or Golden Delicious are recommended)

25g (1oz) butter

60g (2¼ oz) caster sugar

FOR THE SEMOLINA SOUFFLÉ:

500ml (18floz) milk

2 drops vanilla essence or ½ vanilla pod cut in half and scraped

100g (4oz) caster sugar

70g (2¾oz) semolina

70g (2¾oz) sultanas (as pale as you can find them)

4 eggs, separated

TO FINISH THE DISH:

20g (¾oz) unsalted butter

caster sugar for sprinkling

Method:

My mother used to make this dish when I was a child which made me love her ten times over. It's delicious!

It is essential that the apples are pre-baked as this will partly cook them. The apples must be perfectly ripe and I personally find the James Greaves variety to be particularly delicious. Do not peel the apples as the skin will hold their shape, and they will have a nice texture.

Of course, if this dish is for the kids, golden syrup will be welcomed!

1 Planning ahead: The apples must be pre-baked. The semolina can be prepared half an hour in advance and kept warm in a bain-marie (sprinkle with sugar so no crust is formed). Then all you have to do is whip the meringue and incorporate it into the semolina.

2 Preparing the dish: Melt 10g (¼ oz) of the butter and spread a film of it inside a large heatproof dish, then sprinkle with 20g (¾ oz) of the caster sugar. Clean the edge of the dish. Reserve. Preheat the oven to 180°C, 350°F, Gas Mark 4.

3 Pre-baking the apples: Wash the apples and pat dry. Melt the remaining butter and brush over the apples, then coat with the remaining caster sugar. Place on a buttered pastry tray and bake in the oven for approximately 25-30 minutes, according to ripeness. Remove from the oven and reserve.

4 Preparing the semolina soufflé: Bring the milk to the boil together with the vanilla essence (or pod), then lower the heat and add 60g (2¼oz) of the caster sugar, the semolina and sultanas. Simmer for about 3 minutes until the mixture thickens, whisking all the time to prevent any lumps forming or burning the bottom. Cool for 2-3 minutes, and pick out the

Serves 4

Picture Courtesy of Peter Knab, from 'A Blanc Christmas', Headline Book Publishing Ltd

vanilla pod if used.

In a bowl, whisk the egg whites until soft peaks form, and then slowly add the remaining caster sugar. Continue whisking until stiff peaks have been achieved. Mix the egg yolks into the semolina mixture. Briskly whisk in one third of the egg white, then fold the remainder in gently with a spatula.

5 **Baking the soufflé:** Pour the semolina soufflé mixture into the prepared baking dish and imbed the apples in it. Dab a knob of butter on each apple, sprinkle sugar over the dish, and bake in the preheated oven for 25 minutes.

6 **Serving:** Remove the dish from the oven, place it on your table, and let your guests help themselves.

Recipe reproduced by permission from Raymond Blanc's 'Cooking For Friends' (Published by Headline).

Michael Caine

Carrot Cake

Method:

1 Grease and base line 20cm/8in round cake tin.

2 Preheat oven to 180°C, 350°F, Gas Mark 4.

3 Mix butter and sugar until creamy. Sieve together flour, baking powder, cinnamon, ginger and nutmeg. Add one egg to creamed mixture with a little sieved flour. Then mix in carrots with other ingredients.

4 Bake for 1¼-1½ hours.

5 This recipe can be used to make Banana Cake simply by swapping the carrots for bananas.

Ingredients:

2 cups (12oz) light brown soft sugar

8oz butter

4 eggs

4 cups (10oz) plain flour

2 teaspoons baking powder

1 teaspoon ground cinammon

1 teaspoon ground ginger

pinch of ground nutmeg

2 cups (8oz) grated carrots

1 cup (6oz) raisins

1 cup (4oz) chopped walnuts

½ teaspoon vanilla essence

(see photograph on page 77)

Judi Dench

Bread & Butter Pudding

Ingredients:

275ml (½ pint) milk

70ml (2½ floz) double cream

grated rind of half a small lemon

50g (2oz) caster sugar

3 eggs

Pannetone cake

10g (½ oz) candied lemon or orange peel, finely chopped

50g (2oz) currants

freshly grated nutmeg

Method:

Serves 4

This is delicious and provides the perfect solution for what to do with those dry Italian cakes you get given at Christmas!

1 Heat oven to 180°C, 350°F, Gas Mark 4.

2 Butter a 1 litre (2 pint) oblong enamel baking dish. Slice the Pannetone and butter it. Put one layer on the base of the dish, sprinkle with the candied peel and half the currants. Put another layer of Pannetone in the dish and sprinkle with the rest of the currants.

3 Put the milk and cream together in a measuring jug, stir in the lemon peel and sugar. Whisk the eggs in a small basin and add to the milk mixture. Pour the whole lot over the Pannetone and sprinkle with freshly grated nutmeg.

4 Bake in the oven for 30-40 minutes. Serve warm.

Picture Courtesy of Doug Davies, All Action Pictures

Metric & Imperial Equivalents

Comparisons may confuse. Use either metric or imperial measures: do not mix the two.

WEIGHT/SOLIDS		VOLUME/LIQUIDS	
15g	½oz	15ml	½ floz
25g	1oz	30ml	1floz
40g	1½oz	50ml	2floz
50g	1¾oz	100ml	3½ floz
75g	2¾oz	125ml	4floz
100g	3½oz	150ml	5floz (¼ pint)
125g	4½oz	200ml	7floz (⅓ pint)
150g	5½oz	250ml (½ litre)	9floz
175g	6oz	300ml	10floz (½ pint)
200g	7oz	350ml	12floz
225g	8oz	400ml	14floz
250g	9oz	425ml	15floz (¾ pint)
275g	9½oz	450ml	16floz
300g	10½oz	500ml (½ litre)	18floz
325g	11½oz	600ml	1 pint (20floz)
350g	12oz	700ml	1¼ pints
400g	14oz	850ml	1½ pints
425g	15oz	1 litre	1¾ pints
450g	1lb	1.2 litres	2 pints
500g	1lb 2oz	1.5 litres	2¾ pints
600g	1lb 5oz	2 litres	3½ pints
700g	1lb 9oz	2.5 litres	4½ pints
750g	1lb 10oz	3 litres	5¼ pints
1kg	2lb 4oz		
1.25kg	2lb 12oz		
1.5kg	3lb 5oz		
2kg	4lb 8oz		
2.25kg	5lb		
2.5kg	5lb 8oz		
3kg	6lb 8oz		

Spoon sizes

Metric spoon sizes are 15ml, 10ml and 5ml. As these are so close to existing spoon sizes, and in line with European practice, we recommend the continued use of tablespoons, dessertspoons and teaspoons.

For specific help and advice, write with an SAE to The Guild of Food Writers, 48 Crabtree, London SW6 6LW.